# PLACES OF WORSHIP

# Sikh Gurdwaras

Gopinder Kaur

Heinemann
LIBRARY

First published in Great Britain by Heinemann Library
Halley Court, Jordan Hill, Oxford OX2 8EJ
a division of Reed Educational and Professional Publishing Ltd.
Heinemann is a registered trademark of Reed Educational & Professional Publishing Limited.

OXFORD  MELBOURNE  AUCKLAND
JOHANNESBURG  IBADAN  BLANTYRE  GABORONE
PORTSMOUTH NH (USA)  CHICAGO

Designed by Tinstar Design  (www.tinstar.co.uk)
Illustrations by Martin Griffin & Nick Beresford-Davies
Printed by South China Printing in Hong Kong / China

03 02 01 00 99
10 9 8 7 6 5 4 3 2 1

British Library Cataloguing in Publication Data

Kaur, Gopinder
    Sikh Gurdwaras. – (Places of worship)
    1. Temples, Sikh – Juvenile literature
    I. Title
    294.6'35

ISBN 0 431 05186 0

Acknowledgements

The Publishers would like to thank the following for permission to reproduce photographs:
Emmett, Phil, pp. 4, 11, 16, 18; Kaur, Gopinder, pp. 13, 20, 21 (top); Sagoo, Harjinder Singh, pp. 5, 6, 7, 8, 10, 12, 14, 15, 17, 19; Twin Studio, p.21 (bottom).

Cover photograph of Gurdwara Guru Nanak Nishkam Sewak Jatha, Birmingham, reproduced with permission of Harjinder Singh Sagoo.

Our thanks to Philip Emmett for his comments in the preparation of this book, and to Louise Spilsbury for all her hard work.

# Contents

Words printed in **bold letters like these**
are explained in the Glossary.

# What is a Gurdwara?

A Gurdwara is the building where **Sikhs** meet to practise two things: to remember **God** and to help and serve others. Gurdwara means 'at the door of the **Guru**'.

Guru is an Indian word for a teacher or **holy** person. Sikhs use it to describe their ten great teachers and sometimes to describe God. They also use this word for their holy book, the **Guru Granth Sahib**.

The most famous Gurdwara in the world is the Golden Temple, which is in the **Punjab**.

# Sikhs in Britain

Most Sikh families are from the Punjab. Nowadays Sikhs live all over the world. In Britain you can find Gurdwaras in cities such as London, Birmingham, Manchester, Coventry and Leeds.

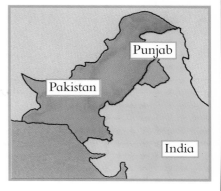

The Punjab is where the Sikh religion began about 500 years ago.

Some Gurdwaras in Britain are in buildings which were once sports centres, or even houses. Others have been specially built.

This Gurdwara in Birmingham was converted from shops and houses.

# Visiting a Gurdwara

As you approach a Gurdwara you might notice people bowing slightly as they enter or leave the building. You may also catch the smell of food cooking, or hear the sounds of dishes clanking. You may hear music and singing, prayers being spoken, or someone giving a talk inside.

This Gurdwara in London was specially built.

# The nishan sahib

Outside every Gurdwara you will see a yellow or orange flag called a **nishan sahib**. On it is the sign of the **khanda**. The shapes on the khanda have a special meaning for Sikhs.

Sikhs prepare to put up the nishan sahib.

## The khanda

On the khanda, the circle reminds Sikhs that there is one supreme **God** and everyone is equal. The sword in the middle stands for freedom and justice. The two swords on each side stand for strength in our everyday life and strength in our **spiritual** life. You might notice the khanda in other parts of the Gurdwara.

# What's inside?

Inside the main entrance of a Gurdwara there is a place for you to take off your shoes and probably a sign saying 'Please cover your head'.
Usually visitors have something to cover their heads with. Women have long coloured scarves, men have **turbans** or, if they don't wear one, they often use a handkerchief to tie over their heads. This is a sign of respect when entering a **holy** place.

Women covering their heads with scarves before going into the Gurdwara.

# The main parts

There are always two main parts to a Gurdwara. The first is the **worship** hall and the second is the **langar** or kitchen area. There may also be a classroom attached to the building. Here children may come to read and write **Punjabi**, learn more about the **Sikh** religion, or have music lessons. In various parts of the Gurdwara you might find pictures of the Sikh **Gurus** and events from Sikh history.

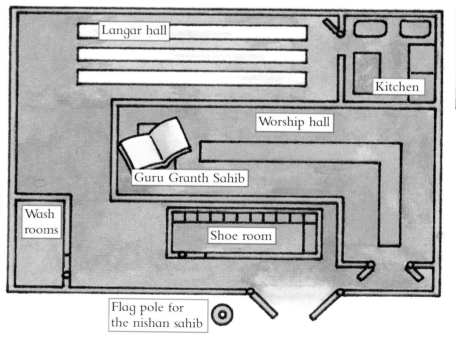

Langar hall

Kitchen

Classroom

Worship hall

Guru Granth Sahib

Wash rooms

Shoe room

Flag pole for the nishan sahib

This is an example of the layout of a Gurdwara.

# The worship hall

In the **worship** hall there is usually a long strip of carpet. It leads from the door to the special raised platform which holds the **Sikh holy** book, the **Guru Granth Sahib**. This is the most important part of the worship hall. People walk along the long carpet and kneel in front of the holy book, to show respect for its teaching.

On one side of the Guru Granth Sahib there is a place for musicians to play, or for someone to give a talk.

People usually sit cross-legged on white sheets in the worship hall.

# The Guru Granth Sahib

The Guru Granth Sahib is treated with a lot of respect, almost as if it were a king or a queen. It is wrapped in beautiful cloths and above it there is a **canopy**. During a **service** someone stands or sits behind it, waving a **chaur**, a kind of fan. This gives it the importance of a royal person.

In front of the platfom is a box. When people come to bow they put money in. This helps with the upkeep of the Gurdwara. Sometimes people bring gifts of food, such as a container of milk or a packet of sugar for the kitchen.

Sikhs bow in front of the Guru Granth Sahib as a sign of respect.

# Who goes there?

Although mostly **Sikhs** go to the Gurdwara, anyone is welcome to come. People who gather together there are called the **sangat**.

In the **worship** hall, the sangat sits on the floor in front of the **Guru Granth Sahib**. Men sit on one side and women sit on the other. Each side has the same amount of space and is on the same level. This shows that man and woman are equal in front of **God**. Young children sit on either side.

The sangat in a Gurdwara.

# Who helps there?

Any Sikh man or woman can look after the Guru Granth Sahib and read from it during a **service**. The person who regularly does this in the Gurdwara is called a **granthi**. A person who has studied the Guru Granth Sahib and can explain its teaching is called a **giani**. The musicians who play and sing **hymns** are called **ragis**.

Anyone who helps out in the running of the Gurdwara is called a **sewadar**. People of all ages help cook, clean or serve in the kitchen, keep the shoes neatly at the entrance or tidy up after a service has finished.

A young Sikh does **sewa** by stacking shoes in special racks.

# What happens there?

**Sikhs** have no special **holy** day in the week, but in Britain most **services** take place at the weekend when many people have time off. In some Gurdwaras, there is a service every morning and evening. The services help Sikhs do two important things: **simran**, which means remembering **God**, and **sewa**, which means serving others.

A popular part of the service is **kirtan**, the singing of Sikh **hymns**. You might also hear the chanting of words, such as Waheguru, which means wonderful **Guru**. Sikhs believe that music helps them feel closer to God. There might also be **katha**, a talk about Sikh teaching.

These children are singing to the **vaja** or harmonium, and the **tabla**, (the two drums).

# At the end of a service

At the end of a service, everyone stands up, folds their hands together and faces the **Guru Granth Sahib**. Then one person leads the **ardas**. The ardas is a prayer in which Sikhs remember the ten **Gurus**, the history of their people, and what they believe in. Then they ask God to **bless** all human beings in the world.

Next, everybody sits down again to listen to the **hukam-nama**. First, the Guru Granth Sahib is opened at any page. Then the verse that appears is read out loud. In this way Sikhs believe that the Guru has given them a teaching to think about.

A man leading the ardas prayer.

# After a service

To mark the end of a **service** in the **worship** hall, **karah parshad** is given to everyone in the **sangat**. A **sewadar** hands out small portions of this sweet mixture from a steel bowl. The sharing of karah parshad is an important sign that everyone is equal in the Gurdwara.

People cup their hands to receive karah parshad.

After an evening service, the **Guru Granth Sahib** is taken away to a special room. The **granthi** says a night-time prayer and a short **ardas**, closes the Guru Granth Sahib, wraps it in special cloths and lifts it over their head. The sangat stands and sings as it is carried away, as if a king or queen is leaving a royal court.

# Langar

The sangat then goes to have **langar**. Langar is food which is served free to everyone who comes to the Gurdwara. In many Gurdwaras people sit in rows on the floor. In this way everyone, rich or poor, sits on the same level and is treated in the same way.

In the langar hall, you can also do **sewa** – help to cook, serve food or wash up dishes. Sometimes a family and their friends prepare langar together. Anyone from the sangat can come and help.

People being served in the langar hall.

# Special events

The Gurdwara is also a place where **Sikhs** come to mark important events in their lives, such as a birthday, a marriage or a death.

## A Sikh marriage

For a marriage, the Gurdwara is full of friends and relatives. The wedding couple sits in front of the **Guru Granth Sahib**, each holding the end of a coloured scarf which links them together. The **granthi** reads out four marriage verses. After each verse, the couple stand up and walk around the Guru Granth Sahib while the **ragis** sing. When they have done this four times the couple are married.

A Sikh couple linked by the special marriage scarf.

# A new baby

When a baby is born in a Sikh family, it is taken to the Gurdwara for the naming ceremony. The Guru Granth Sahib is opened at any page. The first letter of the first verse that appears on that page will be the first letter of the baby's name.

# Tying the first turban

For many Sikhs, keeping long hair is an important **symbol** of being a Sikh. Sikh men with long hair cover it with a **turban**.

When they are young, many boys have their hair tied up in top knots. When they are old enough, they have their first turban tied in a special ceremony at the Gurdwara.

A turban-tying ceremony.

# Festivals

**Gurpurbs** are important **Sikh** festivals. Some celebrate **Gurus'** birthdays. Baisakhi remembers the time in 1699 when the tenth Guru led the first ceremony when Sikhs promised to follow a special way of life. When they live by this promise, they are called the khalsa, which means 'pure ones'.

Gurpurbs usually begin with an **akhand path**, when the Guru Granth Sahib is read non-stop from beginning to end. People take turns to read, and the reading takes two days and two nights. Afterwards there is a big **kirtan** service, with **hymns** and talks to mark the day.

Here Sikhs celebrate a festival outside the Gurdwara with Gatka - a Sikh **martial art** display.

# Children joining in

Children also take part in gurpurb celebrations, by doing kirtan or giving a talk about the Sikh religion. Sometimes they write essays or draw pictures for gurpurb competitions.

If the Gurdwara has a classroom, its walls might be covered with children's work, such as paintings of the Gurus, letters of the **Punjabi** alphabet, or pictures of Sikh **symbols**. One such symbol is the **Ik Onkar**. This reminds Sikhs that there is one supreme **God** and that we are all equal as God's children.

Can you see pictures in the classroom of the Ik Onkar symbol (above)?

# Glossary

The letters in brackets help you to say some words.

**akhand path** (akh–und pARt) the non-stop reading of the Sikh holy book from beginning to end

**ardas** (ar–dARs) prayer said at the end of a Sikh service

**canopy** kind of roof or shade made of material that hangs over a throne or special place

**bless** to bring joy and happiness and make holy

**chaur** (chor) kind of fan that is waved over the Sikh holy book as a sign of respect

**giani** (gy–AAni) person who knows the teachings of the Sikh holy book and can explain them to others

**God** Sikhs believe that God made, sees and knows everything. Sikhs have many different names for God.

**granthi** (grun–thEE) person who looks after and reads from the Sikh holy book

**gurpurb** (gur–purb) Sikh holy day, usually to remember the birth or death of a Guru, or an important religious event

**Guru** (Gur–OO) teacher or holy person. Sikhs follow the teachings of ten Gurus.

**Guru Granth Sahib** (Gur–OO Grunth Saheeb) Sikh holy book, which is now seen as a living Guru

**holy** respected because it is to do with religion

**hukam-nama** (hook–umm–nARma) reading that is taken when the Sikh holy book is opened up at any page

**hymn** a song that is sung in praise of God

**Ik Onkar** (Ik Ong–cAR) important Sikh words meaning there is only one supreme God

**karah parshad** (kur–RAR par–shARd) blessed food, usually a sweet mixture, which is given out after the service to everyone in the Gurdwara

**katha** (kath–AA) talk given about the teachings of the Sikh religion

**khanda** (khun–dAA) Sikh sign with a circle and three swords

**kirtan** (kEER–tun) the singing of hymns from the Sikh holy book

**langar** (lung–er) food that is free to all who come to the Gurdwara

**martial art** fighting skills which train the mind and body

**nishan sahib** (nish–AAn sa–hib) flag which marks the outside of a Gurdwara

**Punjab** place where the Sikh religion began and where most Sikhs come from. Now part of it is in India and part of it is in Pakistan.

**Punjabi** language spoken by people in the Punjab

**ragis** (RAgees) musicians who play hymns in the Gurdwara

**sangat** word for the people who come together at the Gurdwara

**service** meeting to worship God

**sewa** (sometimes spelt 'seva') (say–VA) service to other people

**sewadar** (say–VA–dAR) person who serves others. It comes from the word sewa.

**Sikh** (seek) person who follows the Sikh religion

**simran** (sim–run) remembering God

**spiritual** something to do with the spirit or soul

**symbol** sign with a special meaning

**tabla** two drums which usually accompany the singing of hymns

**turban** length of cloth which is wrapped around the head to cover it. It is usually worn by Sikh men and sometimes by Sikh women.

**vaja** (va–jAA) harmonium, which is played when hymns are sung

**worship** way of remembering and praising God

# Index